Doodles & Me

Stephanie Hazel Evans

@ Stephasocks

ISBN: 9781087457932

To my life partner in crime, Adam.

Thanks for continuously encouraging my ideas,
no matter how strange they might seem!

Foreword by Adam Smith

Hello it's me Adamo! I'm not entirely sure why Steph asked me to write the foreword to her book but it was too much of a huge honour to pass up.
I admit I am nervous, I haven't written anything of substance since school and I hope I can remember how haha.

This book is a wonderful collection of stories and comics from our everyday lives that I hope you will enjoy. If you want to know a secret, this book is a huge step forward for Steph who has always been terrified of publishing and believing in her own art skill (crazy I know!)

She is a huge driving force for me in my art and I know for many of you who have been kind enough to support her in purchasing this book. With this gesture of kindness, you have given immeasurable happiness to a beautiful woman who always thought she would be resigned to making stories but never having the courage to share them with the world. You, today, have changed that for the better.

As you read through this book you will enjoy candid and cute snippets of our lives but also thoughtful musings from a lady so deep and brilliant, it would be criminal for her light to be hidden away from the world.

So please join me in expressing how proud we are of our Steph in her first even published work!

I love you, honey. I have never had such an honour to share my life with someone so different, yet so similar and just so exceptional until the day I met you
x x

(P.S. If this book makes me look like an idiot this is beyond my control, Steph would only let me write the foreword, not edit in all my buff and dashing qualities!)

What is this?

Good question!

It's like a hybrid mix between a book and a comic, I guess I could invent a word for it? "Bomic" ... it doesn't sound very attractive does it. But honestly, I just wanted a little project for myself to have a "creative waffle". I didn't want any set parameters for what can or can't exist here. It's just a place to do what I want to.

You'll see the artwork evolve a lot too. I considered redrawing some of the pictures to make everything more consistent. But there's something charming about leaving that progression for people to see for themselves. I want this to feel like a homemade project and I think if I let myself get too carried away, I'll lose sight of the reason I'm doing it: which is for *FUN*.

Hi! MY NAME IS STEPH.

THIS IS MY
BOYFRIEND
ADAM
AKA THE NICEST
BOI. <u>EVER</u>.

WE ARE VERY IN

LOOOVE

WE HAVE 2 GUINEA PIGS

BUMBLE + CRESTON

AND AN ANGEL PIGGY, BRINDLE.

1.4 KG
(BIG BOI)

THINGS I AM PASSIONATE ABOUT:

DRAWING FACES ON MUSHROOMS

RESCUING SNAILS

FINDING FROGS

CLUNK CLONK

TYPEWRITER SOUNDS

PIXEL ART

BOBBLE HATS

SWATCHING ART SUPPLIES

Books are magical universes

Reading stories and getting lost in someone else's imagination is one of the best feelings in the world. You can walk away from reading a book, feeling like you've spent hours exploring through thick enchanted forests ... or wandering around magical supermarkets (full of blue goblins, that walk backwards and speak entirely in riddles).

In all seriousness though, it's a wonderful way to gain empathy for other people's situations you might not understand too. Almost like a super power that allows you to peek inside someone's else's brain and see what things they think about.

It surprises me whenever I hear someone say that they don't enjoy reading. Considering we live in an age where people are constantly reading social media feeds. We're probably reading now more than ever haha! I reckon they just haven't found the right book that catches their attention (yet!).

Pro tip: replace some social media time with a kindle app on your phone. It's a fun pass time and it's helped my anxiety a lot!

Don't be scared to make something!

I think it's probably obvious by how much I talk about books that they're special to me. I used to write a LOT of stories as a kid, hunched over a typewriter at my Nanny's house. They're some of my most treasured memories.

It feels a shame to admit that I lost touch with reading & writing for a long time. The older I got, the more I lost confidence in my grammar abilities. I started to lean more on just the illustrations to speak because it felt safer than writing something "wrong."

I had an epiphany a while back that's helped change my mindset though. I realised I'm not scared of drawing things "wrong". In fact, I'm sure there's people that spot errors in my work all the time. But it doesn't bother me. Art is subjective, we all know that. Some people love cartoon noodle limbs and others prefer realistically rendered portraits. It's only just hit me that this applies on a much broader scale than just drawing. All kinds of creative fields have this same subjective-ness! Languages are even similar. If you've ever experienced speaking a second language, using entirely grammatically correct sentences isn't that high on the priority scale. As long as you've said something and the other person is able to interpret it, then that's all that matters. Art is just another type of communication. Who cares about spelling mistakes if you've just read and understood an entire story?

Being creative is about creating, not following rules!

Being messy is okay

A huge chunk of the joy I now experience from looking at my childhood typewriter stories, comes from the mistakes. They're covered in scribbles, ink splatters and clumps of white out. It shows a human made it and the thought process that went into creating it. I'm starting to think the quest to make something perfect, only makes it *less appealing.*

MY CHILDHOOD BEARS

BLUE TED
MY FIRST BEAR.
HE'S VERY BEAT UP + OLD.
I WAS SAD HE DIDN'T HAVE A
MOUTH, SO ONE DAY MY NANNY
SEWED ONE ON FOR HIM.
.. PLUS A TONGUE?!
10/10 V. CREATIVE

RED TED
MY SMOLLEST BEAR.
I ONCE LOST HIM ON A
POSTMAN PAT RIDE.
BONUS FACT: HE HAS A **GAP TAG.**
(SUPER TRENDY)

YELLOW TED
THIS IS BLUE TED'S WIFE.
SHE'S BIGGER THAN HIM.
AND HAS A LIGHT UP
RED NOSE.

I USED TO **REFUSE** TO WEAR MY GLASSES

WHAT I'D SEE.

WHAT EVERYONE ELSE WOULD SEE.

I LOVE WEARING MY
GLASSES NOW ·‿·

CLEAR

CIRCLE

THICC

A MEMORABLE DATE

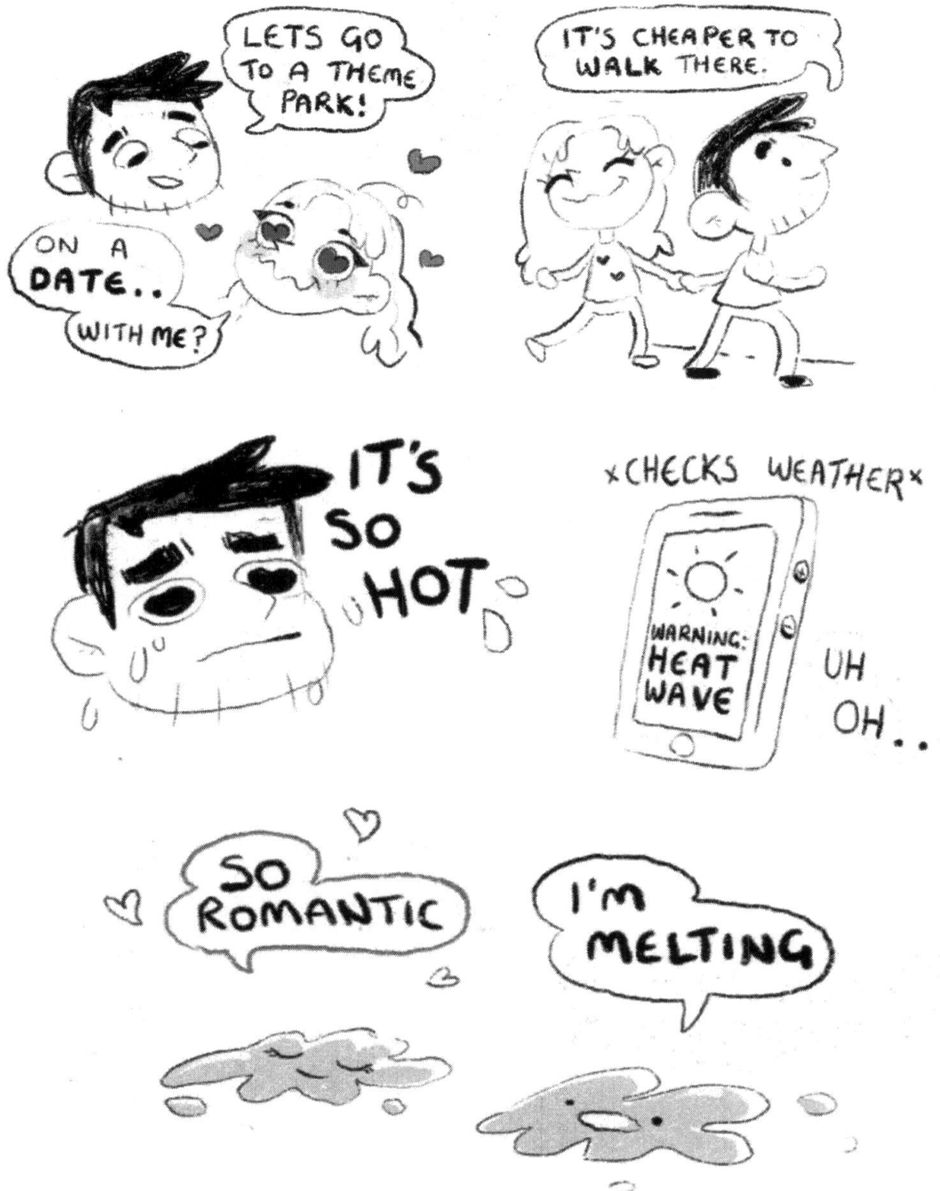
LETS GO TO A THEME PARK!
ON A DATE.. WITH ME?
IT'S CHEAPER TO WALK THERE.
IT'S SO HOT
×CHECKS WEATHER×
WARNING: HEAT WAVE
UH OH..
SO ROMANTIC
I'M MELTING

How did we meet?

This is one of the questions we're both asked the most and it's a fairly long-winded answer, so buckle up.

Long, long ago we were both moderators for an art group called "Cute & Cool". We had the joy of deciding whether submitted artwork fit into either of these two categories. It makes me laugh now because 99.9% of the time I'd just approve the submissions, because I'd spin into a hole of "what even IS cute or cool?" There's no science to help with this classification!

I don't actually remember Adam from this group, but apparently that's how he found me. From my perspective, he mysteriously appeared one day to leave a comment on my profile, saying something along the lines of "hello fellow UK person!" We added each other to our friends lists and would occasionally send each other a comment here and there.

Adam was INCREDIBLY private online. Which might be hard for people to believe now. Back then, he wouldn't disclose a name, gender, age or any telltale signs about who he was IRL. A few online friends used to jokingly call him A.I because they suspected he was an artificial intelligence robot.

Then he vanished for about a year. He'd still occasionally appear online but seemed too busy to interact with anyone. We barely knew each other and our lives went in two separate directions.

My life headed into very rocky terrain as I was nearing graduation at University. I went to a comic convention in London for the weekend to try take my mind off things. *I really struggle with environments like this*, I get bad panic attacks and it usually feels like it wasn't worth the stress. I pushed myself really hard to do it so I could meet up with some online art friends in person. I went dressed in sweet Lolita clothing, I remember I'd recently bought two pairs of the same shoes in different colours, so I could have one of each colour. One in pink and one in black. It seems silly I still remember a detail that insignificant. Later on, I uploaded a photo of my outfit on social media and thought nothing of it. When I went back to check on it, I was surprised to see I had a reply from the mysterious A.I person. I was excited to hear from them again because it'd been so long since we'd last talked. It was so fun catching up and reminiscing about old DeviantArt memories. It wasn't long before we were talking every day and calling each other on Skype. For the longest time he refused to share any photos of himself. Adam didn't come out of his shell overnight but it was so heartwarming watching him slowly allow himself to open up to me. I loved learning about him and still do!

We both have a lot of anxiety which made meeting up in person feel like an impossible challenge. We called things off a few times because we didn't think we'd be able to follow through with it. But somehow, we always ended up talking to each other every day. It became obvious with time how much we really cared for each other.

That's technically the story of "how we first met", although with the nature of us meeting online, it means we've been lucky enough to have two "first meetings."
One online and one in person too!

AT THE ZOO

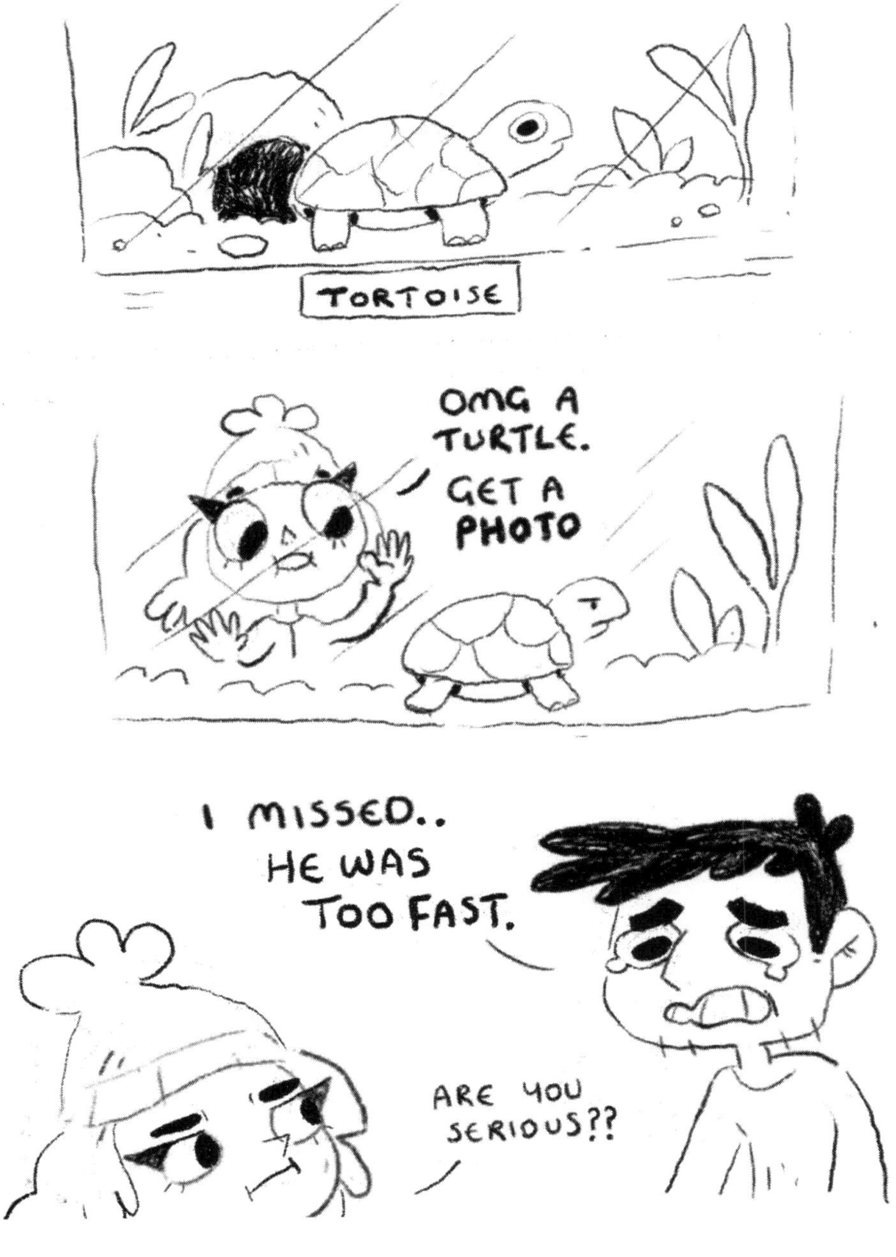
TORTOISE
OMG A TURTLE. GET A PHOTO
I MISSED.. HE WAS TOO FAST.
ARE YOU SERIOUS??

AN EMERGENCY

FAR AWAY
ADAM QUICK IT'S URGENT
OH MY GOD. I THOUGHT YOU WERE DYING!!
SHH.. LOOK. IT'S A FROG.
BIRRRTTt

Fun fact:
This moment had such PERFECT timing IRL.
I'd recently been picked by an author to illustrate one of their books for a pitch, which happened to be entirely about frogs! While on a lunch break with Adam, a frog basically hopped out of the bushes at me. It was fate!

The most special gift

My boyfriend once surprised me with one of the best gifts I've ever been given. He put so much effort into making it that it seriously makes me feel emotional just by looking at it. He filled an *entire* sketchbook with a reason why he loves me on every single page... and there are over 100 pages in this book. It wasn't even my birthday! Although the actual reason he made it for me is so much more sentimental to me than a birthday present.

I'd been going through a lot emotionally and physically with a bunch of doctor appointments. I can still remember so vividly sitting in that doctor's office that day when my doctor told me I'm not well enough to work. I was heartbroken, I'd spent years trying to achieve my goal of working as an artist. It suddenly felt like it was cruelly being ripped away from me. I especially felt terrible for Adam. We work together and it sucks knowing that something beyond your control is going to negatively impact someone you care about. When I got home from that appointment, I crumpled up on the floor crying for hours. Adam gave me so many cuddles and tucked me safely into bed. The next morning, he gave me the book and it honestly brought happy tears to my eyes. He'd been secretly working on it since we'd returned from the doctor's office. It's one of the sweetest things anyone has ever done for me.

ODD THINGS MY BOYFRIEND COLLECTS

INTERNET SHOPPING BUTTON (SERIOUSLY)

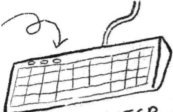

OLD COMPUTER KEYBOARDS

ERASERS

100 YR OLD ART SUPPLIES

VINTAGE PC GAME BOXES

FRIDGE MAGNETS OF PLACES WE'VE BEEN

VERY DATED FASHION BOOKS

BONFIRE SCENTED CANDLES

& LITERALLY ANYTHING FROM MUJI!

A COUPLE'S WALK

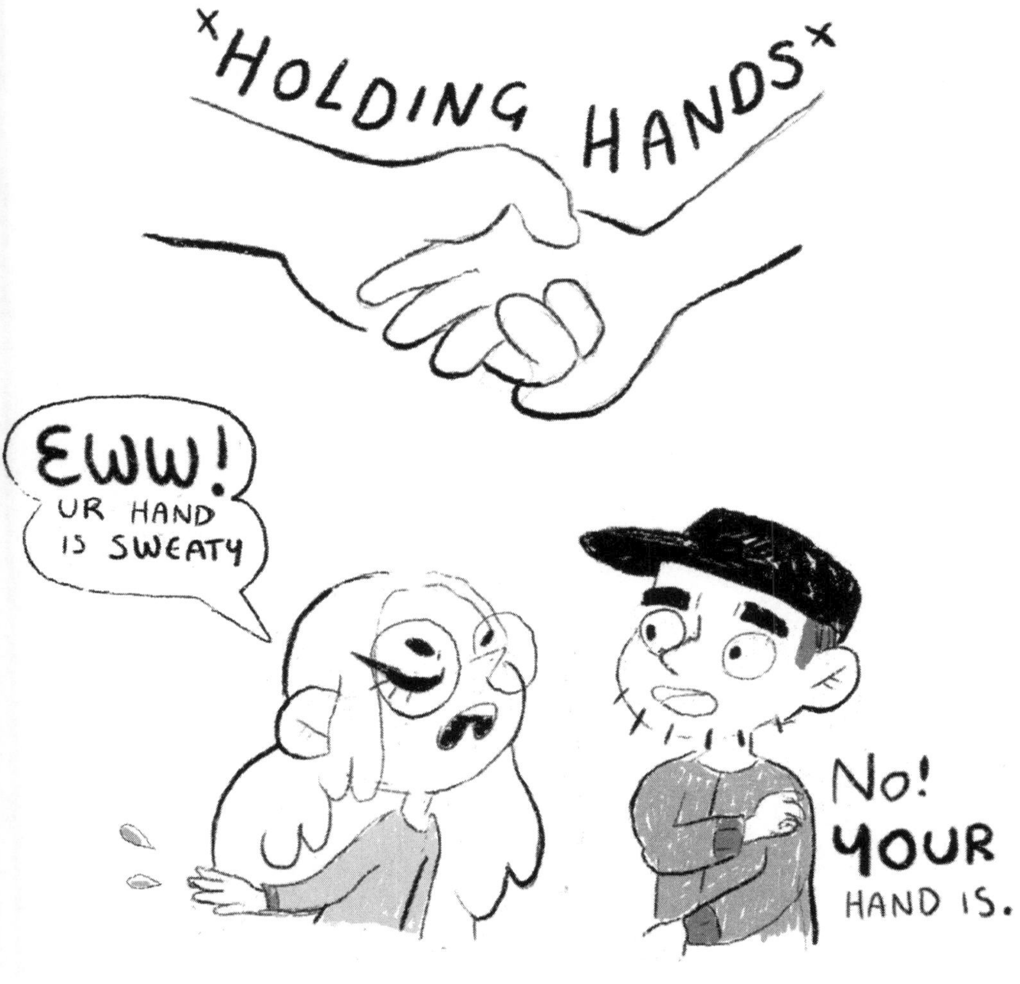
HOLDING HANDS
EWW! UR HAND IS SWEATY
No! YOUR HAND IS.

THINGS I TAKE PHOTOS OF:

PLANTS
B'COS THEY PRETTY

PIGGY PICS
APPROX: 5 BILLION

SNACKS
US IMPORTED POP TARTS

MY ART
USUALLY A MUSHROOM

BOYFRIEND
(RELUCTANT)

CAMERA ROLL

SHARING A YOUTUBE
ACCOUNT WITH MY BF

EXPECTATIONS:

REALITY:

My best friend and colleague!

We have a unique relationship because we get to be #lovers but also working buds. We like spending a lot of time together so we consider ourselves very, very lucky!

Although I'm not sure if I'd be doing YouTube if it wasn't for Adam. My favourite part about making videos is sharing silly experiences with him, I think it's going to be special to watch back over so many of our older adventures together when we're older. Making videos by myself sounds like a much lonelier experience. I don't know how so many of my friends manage to do it?

I love, love, love how many different memories I have stored with Adam, we have what feels like an infinite number of photos, videos, sketches and comics!

Memories are special

I'm totally over sentimental about storing memories. Growing up I lost the majority of my childhood pictures and home movies. It almost feels like I don't have evidence that I used to be a real kid, plus my memory gets foggier with age which makes it harder to remember things very well. Don't underestimate the power of a photo, even if it is a sucky-pixelated-potato-webcam-quality one.

To conquer this, I have a little sketchbook where I store all my favourite memories of relatives and friends that have passed away. It's all messily jotted down in scribbly text and doodles. The importance is to quickly get the ideas recorded on paper, not to make them pretty. When it's in my head, I run the risk of losing it. It feels safer keeping them tucked away inside a book I can easily access!

OUR COMICS

UNA   FJARI   HUNNI   KOKO

UNA

CEREAL FAIRIES

Comics

My boyfriend's been working on a comic called Una for a few years. One of the parts that was particularly slowing him down was the colouring process. He's colourblind so it's a bit trickier for him than it is for most people! I volunteered to colour the second half of the story to help him out. I did it as a helpful gesture to try give him more time to focus on the bits he enjoyed, although I ended up taking away a lot more from the experience than I expected. It made me think of being a school kid doing works experience again haha! (Except way more interesting than my actual work experience, I had to sit in a magistrate's court for a day and I wasn't allowed to talk.)

I also have my own personal comic too called Cereal Faeries. It was meant to be a small project that I'd throw together quickly to get a feel for making a graphic novel. But yikes it evolved into something much bigger than anticipated – like most of my ideas, ha. That's why I'm currently making this book! Instead of jumping into the deep end, I'm forcing myself to work on something smaller scale with an end goal attainably within sight. I still intend to finish my Cereal Fairies comic but it's nice getting some experience under my belt first.

You've probably noticed by now that this book is all in black & white. Colouring takes a lot of time so I had the brainwave that working in b&w allows me to draw and finish things faster. Plus, it also gives me Inktober nostalgia (an art challenge where you draw using ink everyday in October.)

IMAGINATION
IS A FORM OF MAGIC

OUR FIRST DATE

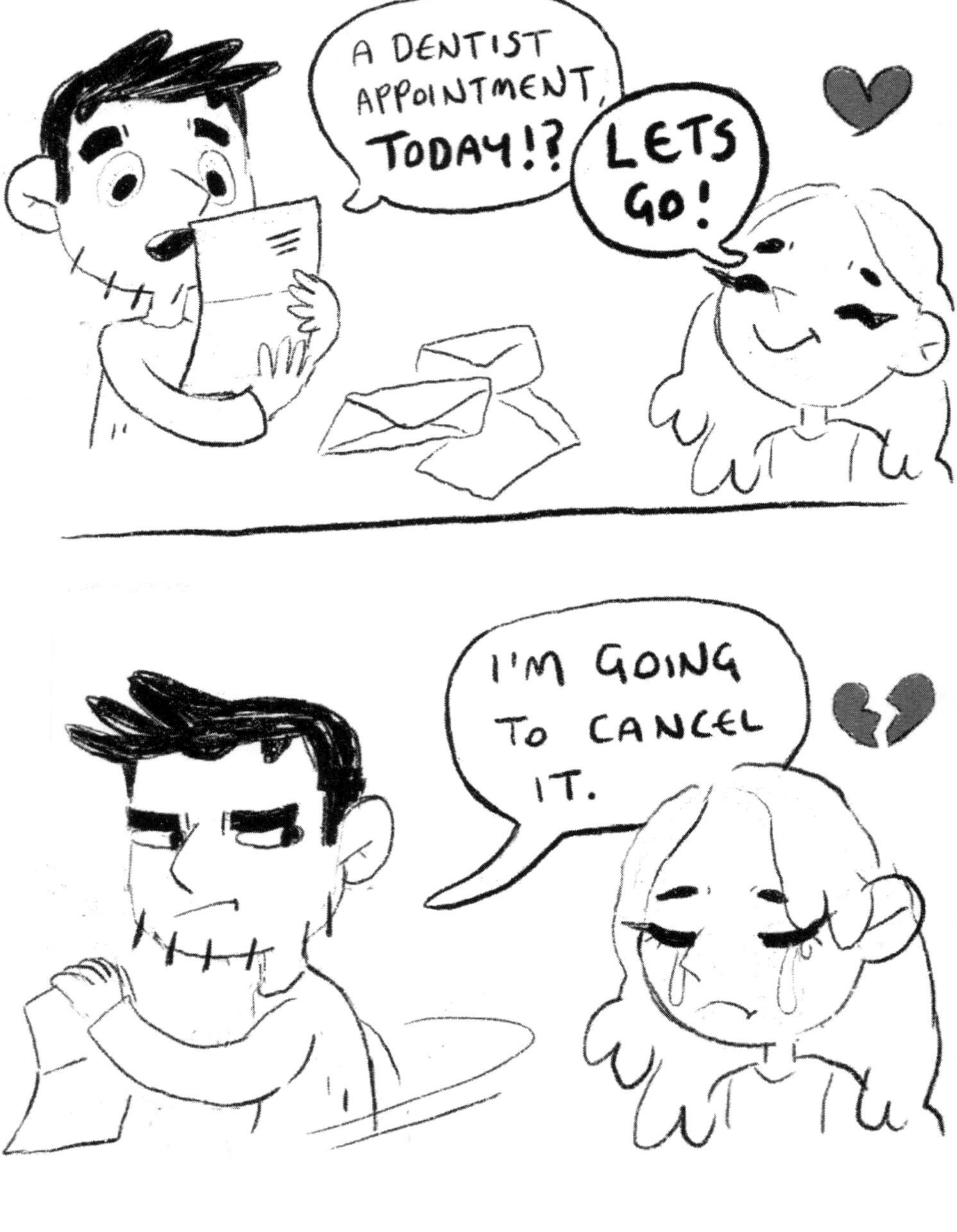
A DENTIST APPOINTMENT, TODAY!?
LETS GO!
I'M GOING TO CANCEL IT.

FACTS ABOUT MY BF:

1. HE HAS THE BEST **SMILE**

2 HE WALKS PAST PARKS TO LOOK FOR **POOCHIES**

3 THIS SMELLS

HE TAKES CARE OF THE **STINKY** CHORES.

Things I have learnt about Adam:

1) He has the best smile, EVER. I used to beg him to send me photos of what he looked like in person. For a while he'd only send me close ups of his teeth! The joke was on him because I thought it was a very nice smile.

2) He will always walk through a pooch park. it doesn't matter whether it means adding a substantial amount of time to a journey. If there's a way he can route a day out past a dog park, then he's going to do it.

3) He's the master of unclogging our washing machine. The tenant that used to live here let us buy her washing machine for only £10, we thought it was an amazing bargain because we were a broke young couple. But heck, over the years I can definitely see why this machine was so reduced. I hope one day we can get a nicer one, but also, they're expensive and I can't stomach forking out for one.

4) He loves jelly sweets, particularly Haribo. If he offers you one, take it immediately. It won't be there in another 10 minutes.

5) Whenever I get new fluffy bed socks, he insists he also needs to wear a pair otherwise he'll feel left out!

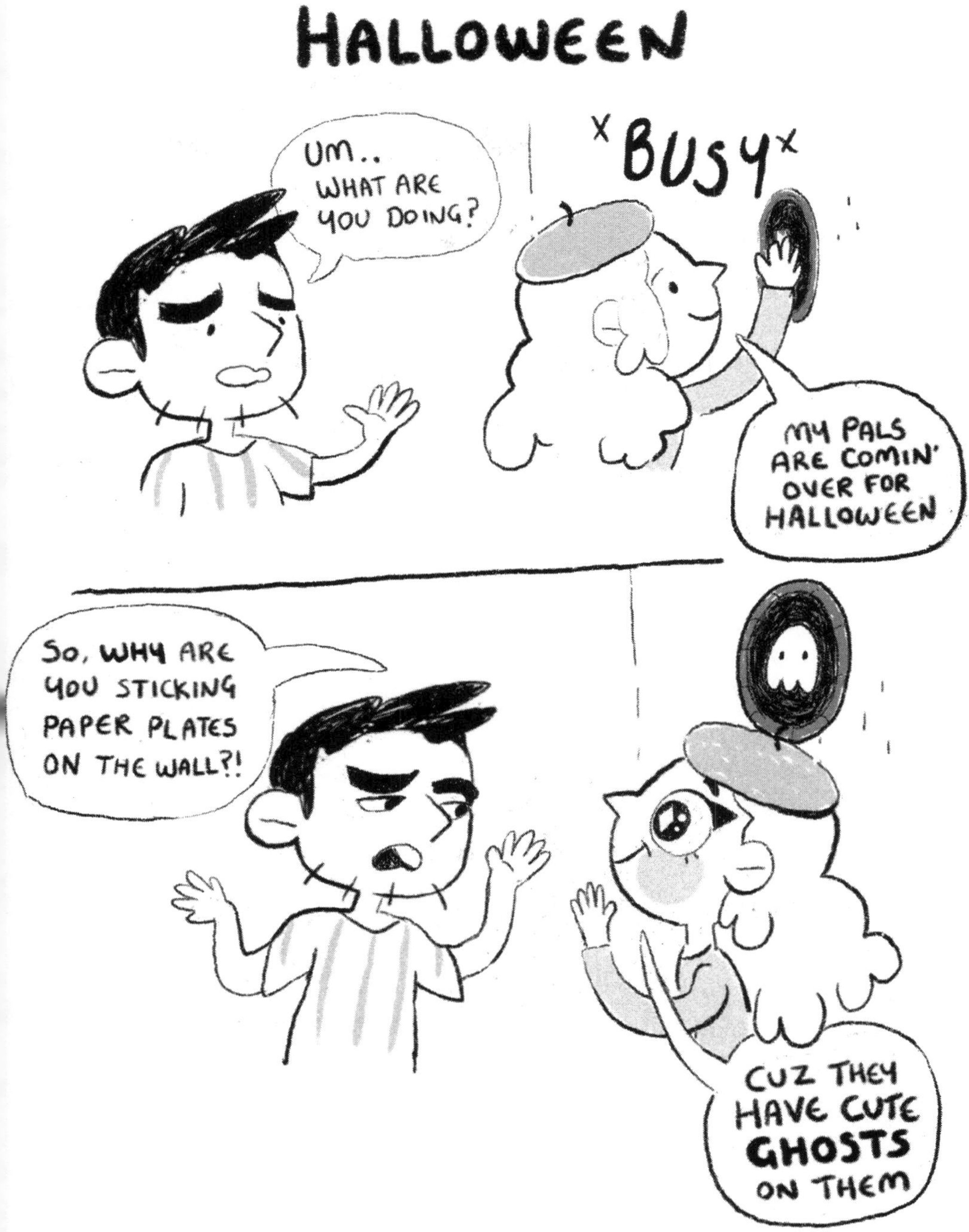
HALLOWEEN
UM.. WHAT ARE YOU DOING?
BUSY
MY PALS ARE COMIN' OVER FOR HALLOWEEN
SO, WHY ARE YOU STICKING PAPER PLATES ON THE WALL?!
CUZ THEY HAVE CUTE GHOSTS ON THEM

HOW I EDIT VIDEOS

✗ SAVES CUTE SCREENSHOTS ✗

HOW MY BF EDITS VIDEOS

BEFORE → AFTER

REGULAR
HUMAN

*DISTORT,
ZOOM*

About the Author

Stephanie Hazel Evans is a British illustrator living in England with her partner. They both share a YouTube & Twitch channel called DoodleDate.

Social media

- My Twitter & Instagram: @Stephasocks

- YouTube & Twitch: DoodleDate

- Shared Instagram account: @doodledateofficial

- My boyfriend's Twitter & Instagram: @Adamsketches

- Support our work over on Patreon: DoodleDate

Made in the USA
Columbia, SC
27 December 2022

75054768R00024